Humpity-Bump!

By Joëlle Murphy
Illustrated by LeeLee Brazeal

ScottForesman
A Division of HarperCollins*Publishers*

Over the leaf,
humpity-bump.

Under the nest,
humpity-bump.

Down the tree,
humpity-bump.

Through the grass,
humpity-bump.

Up the stem,
humpity-bump.

6

In the cocoon,
humpity-bump.

Away I go.
Look at me!